W9-COE-114

USBORNE FIRST READING
Level Three

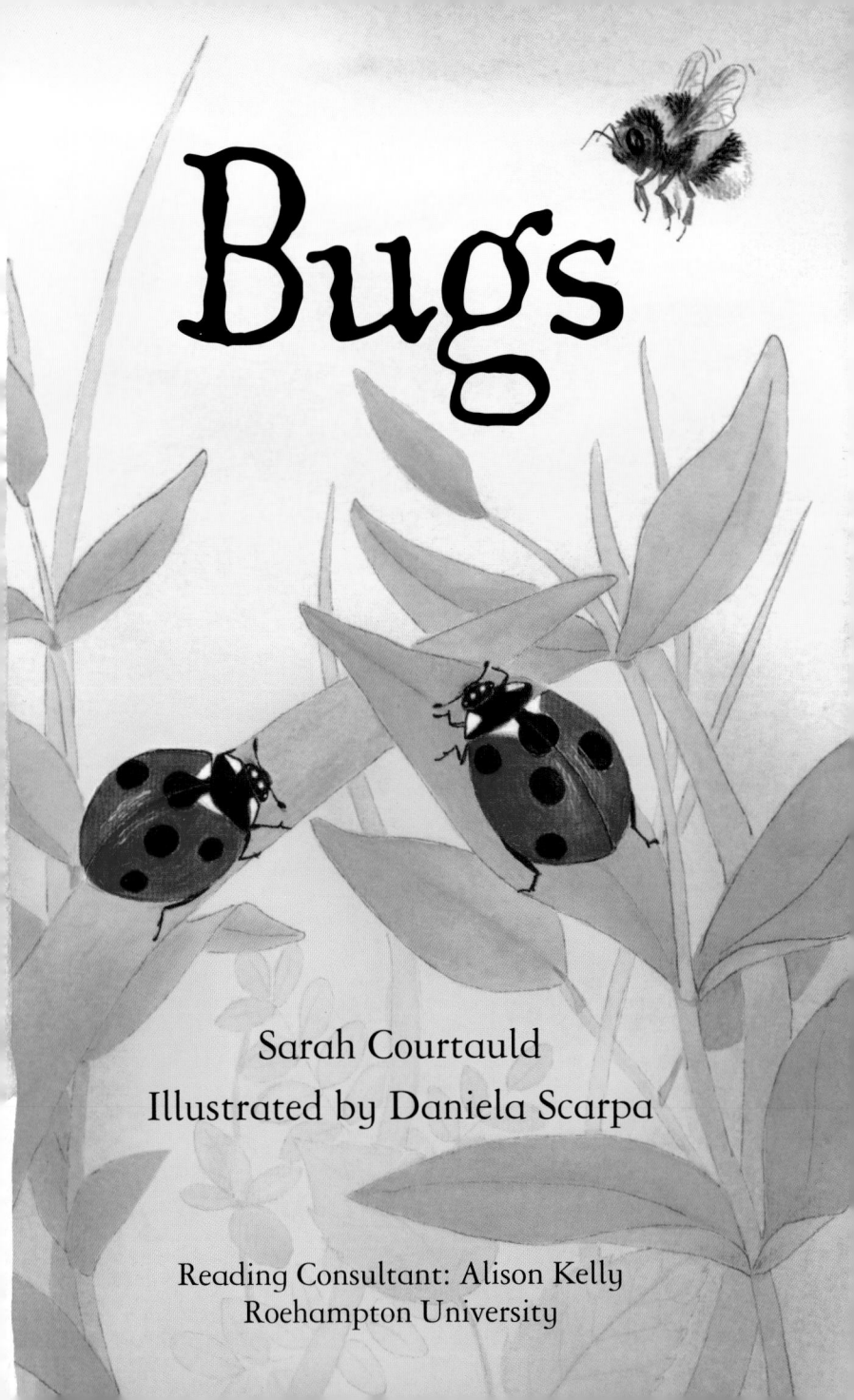

Bugs

Sarah Courtauld
Illustrated by Daniela Scarpa

Reading Consultant: Alison Kelly
Roehampton University

Wherever you look...

...you can find lots and lots of creeping, crawling animals called bugs.

There are millions of different kinds of bugs.

Shiny beetles,

hairy spiders,

buzzing
dragonflies,

furry
caterpillars...

and many,
many more.

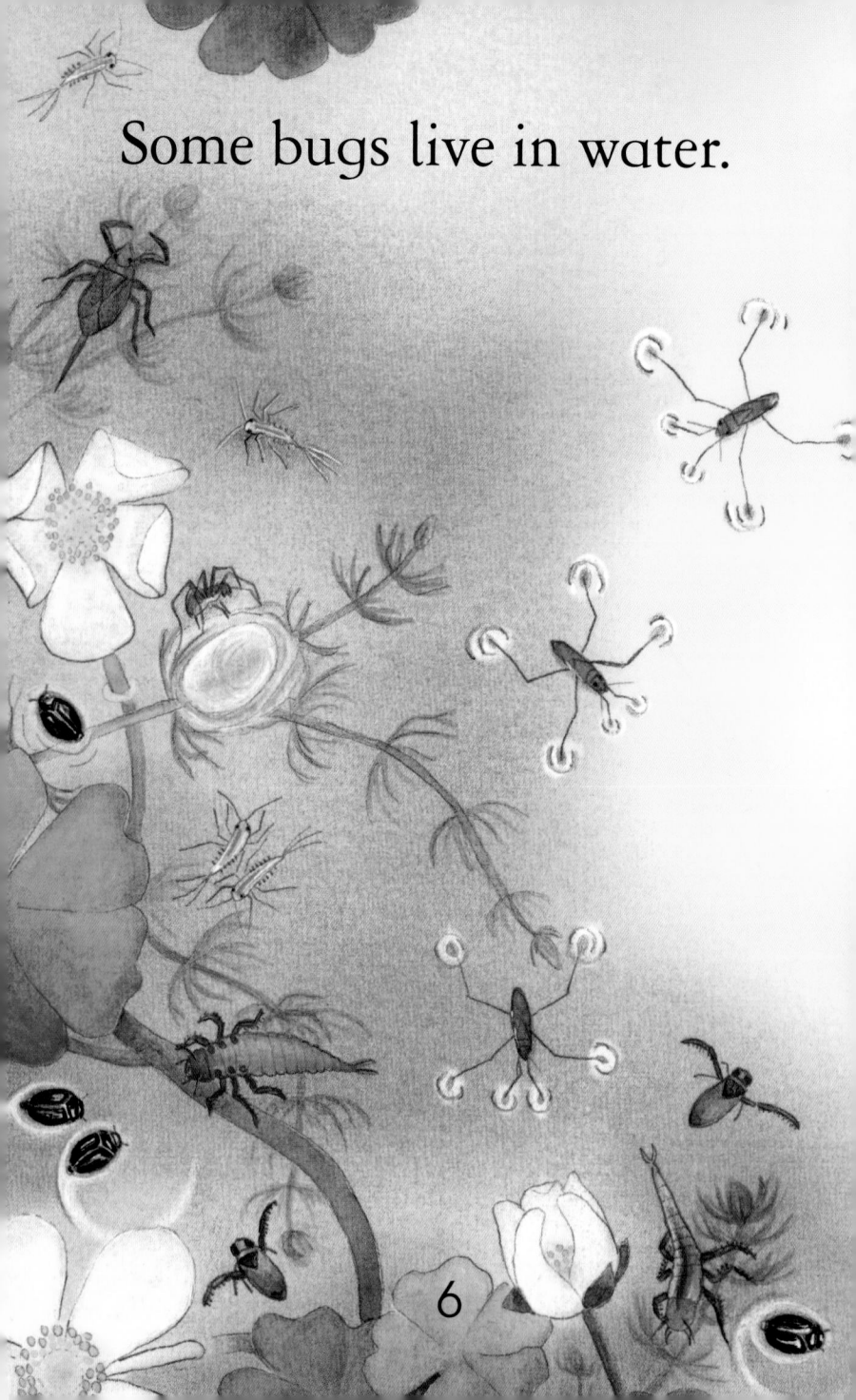

Some bugs live in water.

Some flutter
through the air.

And some bugs live all alone in holes in the ground.

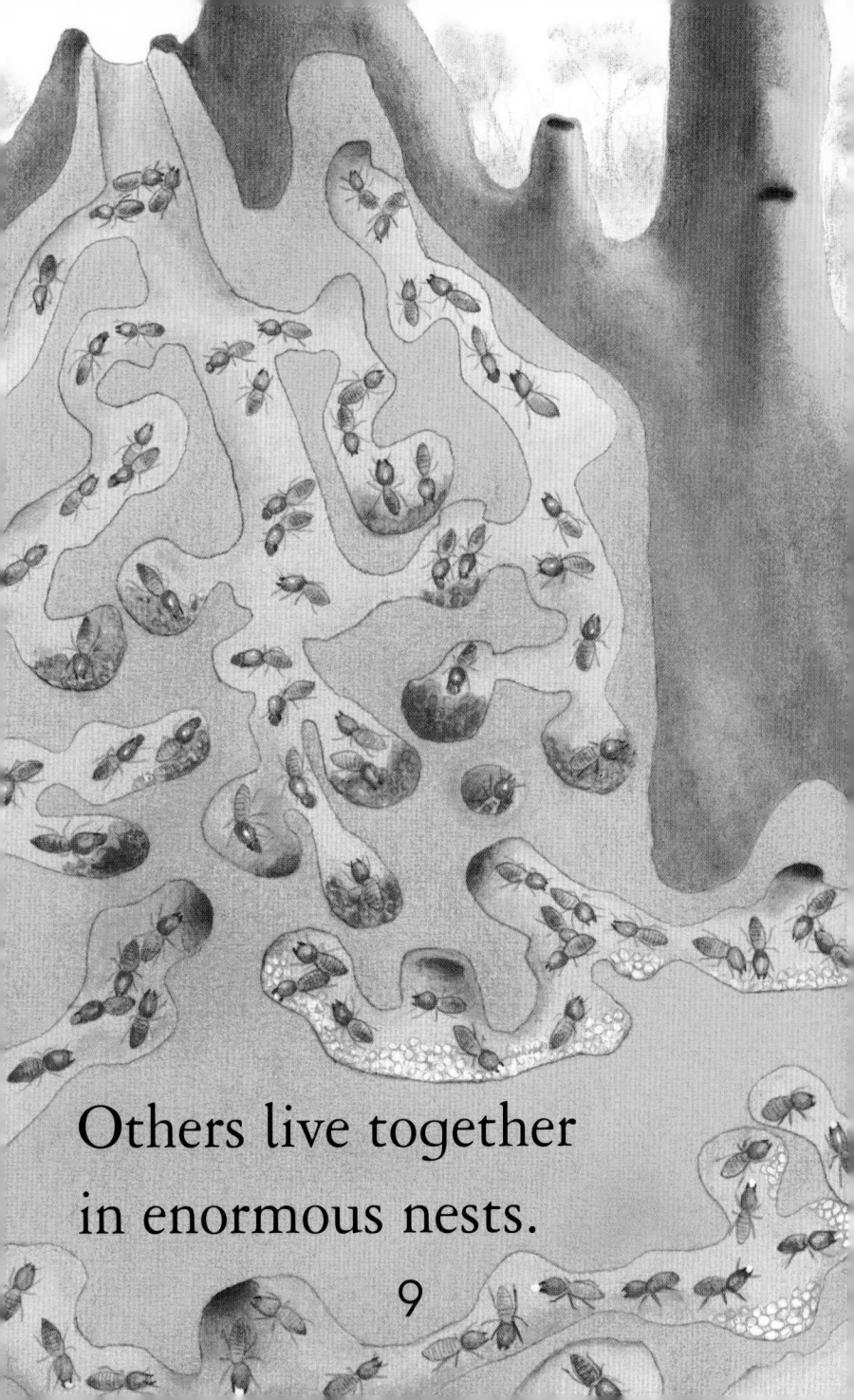

Others live together
in enormous nests.

There are
bugs as long
as your arm

and bugs that
are almost too
small to see.

A blade of grass looks like
a huge tree to a tiny bug...

...but these tiny bugs can
leap far above the grass

up, up, up

into the air.

Many bugs have hard shells. All bugs have six legs or more.

Spiders have eight legs.

Centipedes have dozens of wriggly legs.

Many bugs have
big eyes.

But they don't see what we see. This is how the world looks to a bee.

Bugs find their way around with long feelers.

They smell things with their feelers too,

and find tasty food.

Leaf cutter ants smell leaves with their feelers.

They pick them up and carry them home to eat.

Bees make their own food.
They suck sugar from
flowers...

and carry it
back to their hive.

Then they turn the sugar
into honey to eat

and save it
up for winter.

Some bugs eat other bugs.
A spider spins a long,
silky web.

A fly buzzes into the
web and gets stuck.

The spider gobbles up the juicy fly.

Other animals eat bugs too. But bugs use tricks to escape.

This bug looks just like a leaf.

A bird is looking for bugs
to eat. It can't see any.

The bug stays still
and the bird flies away.

Birds like eating
caterpillars...

...but not this one.
It has big red spikes.

The sharp spikes don't look good to eat.

The bird flies off and the caterpillar is safe.

Bugs grow up fast. Then they rush out to find a partner.

Grasshoppers find partners by rubbing their legs.

This makes a noise that goes chirrup chirrup

so other grasshoppers find them.

Fireflies find a partner by shining. They glow like little stars.

The males fly to the females...

and they get into pairs.

Wolf spiders find a partner by dancing. But they have to be careful. If they make a wrong move...

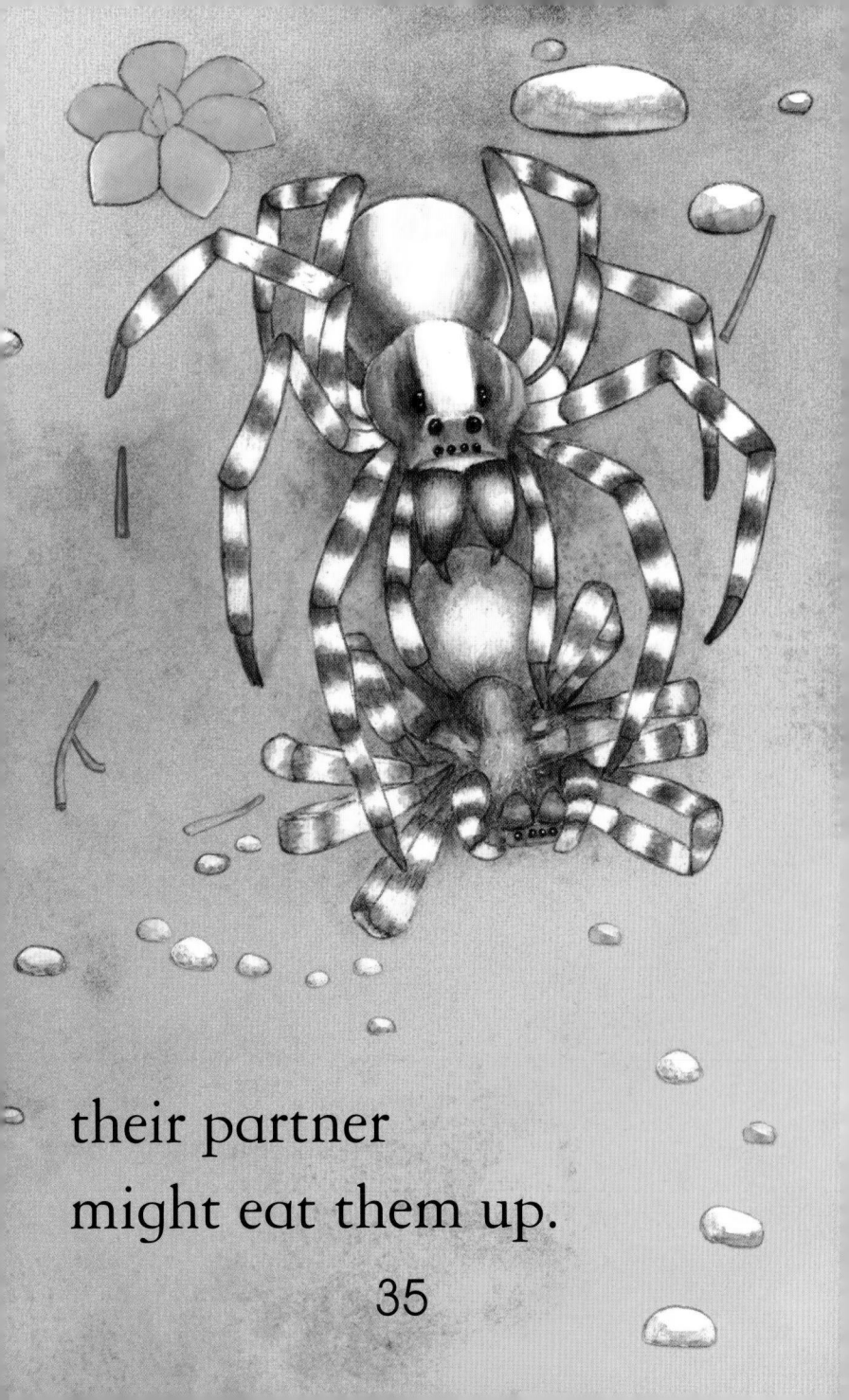

their partner
might eat them up.

Once the bugs are in pairs, the female bug lays lots of eggs.

Butterflies don't take care of their eggs.

They fly off right away.

When baby bugs are born, they are very, very hungry.

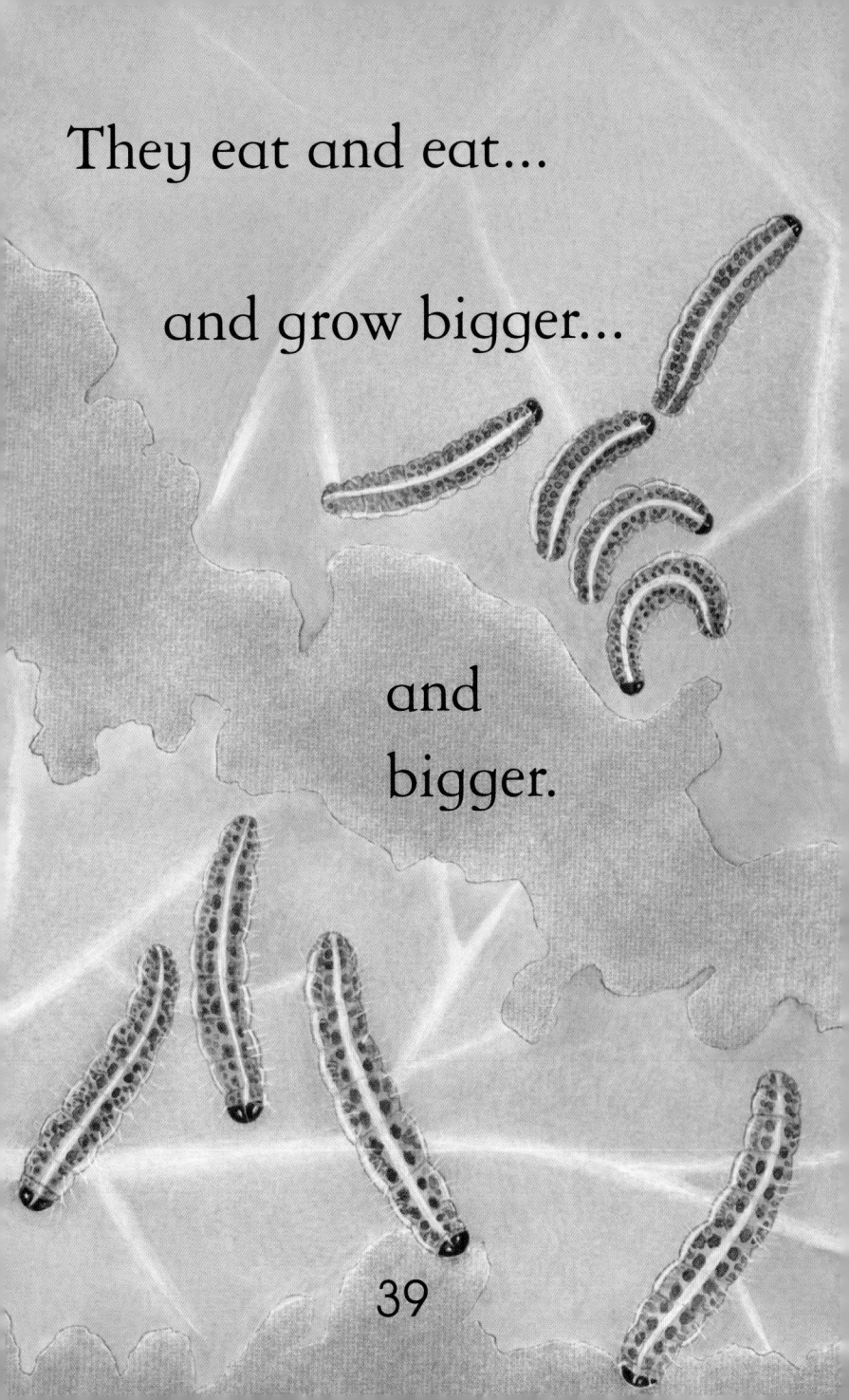

They eat and eat...

and grow bigger...

and
bigger.

These bugs have grown
too big for their shells.

They burst
out of them.

There are shiny,
new shells underneath.

Some bugs change shape as they grow. Dragonflies are born underwater.

They grow larger and crawl onto land.

They shed
their skins

and soar
into the air.

There are wriggling, leaping and flying bugs all around you.

Look outside.
How many can you see?

Bug words

Here are some of the words in the book you might not know.

hive - a place where bees live

web - a silk net made by a spider

feelers - long stalks on a bug's head

Index

eggs, 36-37
eyes, 16-17
feeding, 19-25, 35, 38-39
feelers, 18-20
flying, 7, 32-33, 43
nests, 9
shells, 14, 40-41
water bugs, 6, 42

Bug websites

You can find out more about bugs by going to the Usborne Quicklinks Website at www.usborne-quicklinks.com and typing in the key words "first reading bugs". Then click on the link for the website you want to visit.

The recommended websites are regularly reviewed and updated but, please note, Usborne Publishing is not responsible for the content of any website other than its own. We recommend that young children are supervised while on the internet.

Edited by Susanna Davidson

Designed by Katrina Fearn

Series editor: Lesley Sims

Consultant: Matt Shardlow,
Director of Buglife,
The Invertebrate Conservation Trust

First published in 2007 by Usborne Publishing Ltd., Usborne House, 83-85 Saffron Hill, London EC1N 8RT, England. www.usborne.com
Copyright © 2007 Usborne Publishing Ltd.

All rights reserved. No part of this publication may be reproduced, stored in a retrieval system or transmitted in any form or by any means, electronic, mechanical, photocopying, recording or otherwise, without the prior permission of the publisher. The name Usborne and the devices are Trade Marks of Usborne Publishing Ltd.
Printed in China. UE. First published in America in 2008.

USBORNE FIRST READING
Level Four

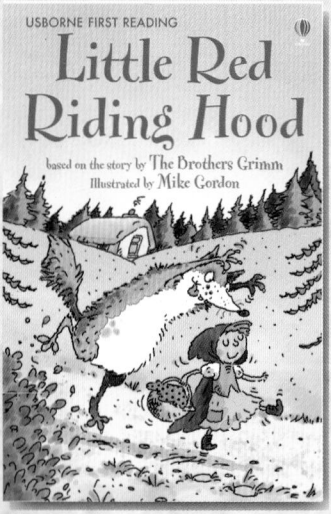